T0244638

THE PHILOSOPHY OF
CIDER

THE PHILOSOPHY OF
CIDER

JANE PEYTON

BRITISH LIBRARY

First published 2024 by
The British Library
96 Euston Road
London NW1 2DB

ISBN 978 0 7123 5505 6
eISBN 978 0 7123 6852 0
Cataloguing in Publication Data
A catalogue record for this book is available
from the British Library

Designed and typeset by Sandra Friesen
Printed in the Czech Republic by Finidr

CONTENTS

INTRODUCTION

Rethink Cider

MY FIRST EXPERIENCE of drinking alcohol was as a child during Christmas dinner, when I had a mouthful of cider. It was sweet, bubbly and delicious. I assumed all cider tasted like that, so as a teenager I was surprised to come across dry, still scrumpy. The day following this latter encounter was memorable for all the wrong reasons, and I'm sure that's why countless people use the excuse 'I never touch cider, it gave me a terrible hangover when I was 15' to avoid drinking it as adults. I have no doubt they have since felt the aftermath of other boozy sessions, but something causes them to abandon cider entirely.

In Britain, where I was born, cider has a negative connection with street drinkers necking cheap industrially produced hooch from which all natural characteristics of the apple have been removed. Consequently, cider has a low value perception, and yet if more people knew that at its best it is the equivalent of fine wine, they might be

1

more respectful. Wine is made by pressing grapes, then fermenting and maturing the juice. Cider is made by pressing apples, then fermenting and maturing the juice. The problem is that cider has no legal definition so, as well as being artisan or farmhouse-style made of fresh apple juice, it can also be a beverage produced from a minimum of juice concentrate (in some countries from no juice at all) where water, sugar, flavourings, colourants and preservatives complete the list of ingredients and connection with an apple tree is fleeting.

But good cider is sunlight in a glass, the liquid expression of the orchard's soul. It fascinates me so much I studied to become an accredited pommelier, and by doing so entered a parallel universe known as Ciderland, a rural realm where nature rules, life is slow, and time is dictated by the growing season. In this book Ciderland refers to the places that produce minimal-intervention cider from fresh apple juice, also termed artisan, farmhouse or real cider, as opposed to cider made from juice concentrate. I wish there were individual terms for both philosophies to avoid customer confusion – 'ciderita' for the latter perhaps?

Of all alcoholic drinks, cider is the most misunderstood. A few years ago I was chatting with Susanna Forbes, co-founder of Little Pomona Cidery, and we discussed how the majority of people have no idea cider is anything other than a mass-market sweetened fizzy beverage. We agreed it would benefit from some reputation management and

TRADE MARK

came up with the hashtag RethinkCider. This has become a rallying call used by evangelists around the world to spread the good news and convert people one glass at a time.

Some traditionalists are suspicious of the artisan cider movement or cider being described as wine-like. Perhaps they are concerned no-frills farmhouse cider will be threatened, but rather than diminish it, enthusing and using language familiar to wine-drinkers encourages more people to understand and appreciate real cider, and may even inspire them to travel up a leafy lane to purchase a flagon from the farmer.

Each cider culture has its own distinct story, but as Britain is the world's largest producer, parts of this book are UK-centric. Cider has a fascinating tale which cannot be told without also focusing on apples. The ancient history of apples and cider is scattered with 'maybe', 'possibly' and 'perhaps' because few archaeological remains exist, and written evidence is paltry and often confusing. There is also the issue of the etymology of 'cider', from *shekar*, Old Testament Hebrew for 'strong drink', which entered Latin as *sicera*. Neither referred explicitly to a fermented apple drink. There was no specific term for cider, and Roman naturalist and philosopher Pliny, when expounding on what he described as 'artificial wine' (i.e. not from grapes), wrote that it could be made 'of all kinds of apples', but in his time that word did not just apply to what we now classify as an apple, namely *Malus pumila*.

Ciderland is global and exists in tracts around Britain, particularly Herefordshire, Worcestershire, Gloucestershire, Somerset, Devon, Cornwall, Kent, Sussex and Monmouthshire; Ireland; northern Spain in Asturias and the Basque Country (straddling the Spanish–French border); Normandy and Brittany in France; Germany's Saarland and Hessen regions; and Austria. It is found in the Norwegian region of Hardangerfjord; in pockets of Sweden, Latvia, the Italian Tyrol and the Netherlands; on the Japanese island of Honshu; in the USA, especially in New Hampshire, Vermont, New York, Michigan and the Pacific Northwest; and in the Canadian provinces of Ontario and Quebec. In the southern hemisphere

Ciderland is in South Africa's Western Cape; the Australian states of Victoria, New South Wales and Tasmania, which is nicknamed Apple Isle; and it nestles within some of New Zealand's vineyards. Depending on apple variety, traditions and methods, a panoply of cider iterations awaits, from the driest, most acidic to the unctuously sweet; rough scrumpy to barrel-aged vintage; still and sparkling; soft or firm tannins; light to full bodied; young or mature. With food it enhances a casual curry and a distinguished banquet equally. It is a refreshing long drink, an elegant Champagne-style fizz served in a flute, or a sipping brandy after dinner. If cider were human, it would need therapy for its multiple personalities!

Maybe this book will convince the not already converted to explore artisan cider and become an advocate too, in which case a paradise awaits where cider made with freshly pressed juice slowly ages in oak or chestnut barrels, and cideristas gather for good times.

A IS FOR APPLE

WHOEVER COINED THE phrase 'the humble apple' must surely be unaware of the epic journey of *Malus sieversii* and *Malus sylvestris*, the wild ancestors of today's cultivated *Malus pumila*, from their home in the foothills of Central Asia's Tien Shan mountains to six of the world's seven continents. With more than 7,500 cultivars apples are ubiquitous, and it is hard to imagine a fruit bowl without one, but how did the apple become one of the most widely consumed fruits?

Animals, birds and nomadic humans ate apples and distributed pips in dung or through discarded cores. If a pip happened to germinate and mature into a tree and the blossom was pollinated, then fruit would grow, which in turn was eaten by animals, birds and humans, thereby extending the range, especially with migration from Central Asia starting around 50,000 years ago. Being solid fruit with protective skin, apples were portable food that travelled well. With the domestication of horses in the Eurasian steppes and the opening of transnational trade routes, apple territory extended to China, the Middle East, the Black Sea

and Europe. The oldest archaeological remains of wild apples are in Turkey, dating to 6500 BCE, and the Basque region, from 5580 BCE. A precise timescale for the domesticated apple is unclear, but agriculture emerged *circa* 10,000 BCE when some humans changed from being wandering hunter-gatherers and settled in one place to tend crops. Apples do not reproduce to type, so each pip is a new variety rather than a clone and may not have the same qualities as its mother. Not all apples are palatable, some are too sour or bitter, but with the development of grafting, probably in China or Mesopotamia (Iraq) around 4,000 years ago, selective breeding made it possible to recreate toothsome varieties. Grafting entails fusing a bud cutting from the desired tree onto root stock so it unites with the surrogate parent, transfers genetic material and grows into a plant. This procedure bypasses the seedling stage, so trees bear fruit years sooner, and today it is still the foundation of apple agronomy.

As knowledge of the technique spread, so did cultivation of an assortment of fruit trees. Roman mosaics discovered in Turkey and France depict scenes of apples and grafting. Theophrastus, a Greek scholar in the fourth century BCE often described as 'the father of botany', wrote about how grafting resulted in superior fruit to that grown from seed. Apples thrive in temperate climates with cool winter conditions because they need a period of cold temperatures in their growing season for the most fulsome blossom, and thus in the Roman territories of Britain, Germany, Austria, Normandy, Brittany and northern Spain, apples flourished. Today they are the heartlands of cider production.

Colonisation, trade and exploration disseminated ideas, practices and produce. The durability of apples made them ideal sustenance for long journeys. Between the sixteenth and eighteenth centuries Europeans took apple trees to plant in the lands they occupied overseas: Spanish

THE POMMEPENDIUM

Of the *circa* 7,500 apple cultivars worldwide, hundreds are specifically grown to produce cider, from Amere de Berthecourt to Zabergau Reinette. Apples that grow from seed rather than by grafting are gribbles or pippins (from Anglo-Norman French *pepin*, for seed). Yarlington Mill, widely considered to be one of the greatest cider apples, was a nineteenth-century gribble discovered in Somerset.

Apples are classified according to levels of acidity and tannins. Malic acid is the source of the tang, and tannins give structure, body, complexity and balance. The categories are:

BITTER: high tannins

BITTERSHARP: high tannins and acidity

BITTERSWEET: high tannins and sugar, low acidity

SHARP: high acidity, low tannins

SEMI-SHARP: medium acidity, low tannins

SEMI-SHARP-BITTER: medium acidity and tannins

SWEET: high sugar, low tannins and acidity

Some apple superstars, such as Kingston Black, possess the Holy Trinity, a perfect combination of acidity, tannins and sugars, and suit being single-variety ciders.

Arguably the most evocative apple names are Slack Ma Girdle, possibly for the cider's effect on the digestive system; Sops in Wine, after pink spots on the apple flesh which look like droplets of wine; and Ten Commandments, named for ten red dots spaced evenly around the core.

conquistadors in Chile and Argentina (where apple is now the national fruit); English settlers in the American colonies; French colonists in Canada; and the Dutch East India Company in South Africa's Cape territory. William Bligh, captain of HMS *Bounty* (the infamous mutiny happened later on the same voyage), planted seven apple trees on Tasmania's Bruny Island. He returned four years later and recorded in his log that one of the trees had survived and the fruit was green and tasted slightly bitter. Together this was the foundation of the modern-day apple-growing industry.

Apples may not be the world's number-one consumed fruit – that accolade goes to tomatoes – but of all fruits it arguably has the most significance in culture, and features in language, literature, art, music, business and science:

- In idioms it appears as 'A is for apple', 'You are the apple of my eye', 'The apple does not fall far from the tree', 'An apple for the teacher' or 'One bad apple spoils the whole barrel'.
- Isaac Newton's observation of an apple falling from a tree inspired the theory of gravity, although the fruit hitting him on the head is probably a legend.
- Impressionist painter Paul Cezanne said, 'With an apple I want to astonish Paris', and his apple still-lifes are among his most celebrated works. René Magritte's *The Son of Man* is the instantly recognisable image of a man in a bowler hat with a green apple for a face. Magritte produced another work, *Le Jeu de Morre*, featuring a green apple inscribed with the phrase 'Au revoir'. Paul McCartney purchased the painting and it is the reason Apple is the name of the Beatles' media corporation.
- The title of the world's most valuable company may have been inspired by co-founder Steve Jobs' visit to an apple farm, although multiple sources claim it was borrowed from the Beatles' company moniker.

Prior to the botanical classification of fruit in the eighteenth century, written references to apple(s) have a caveat because previously the word was a term for fruit in general and not specifically used to describe *Malus pumila*, so any mention of apples in writing is inconclusive as to which

GLASS APPLES

In medieval Germany, town guilds staged yuletide paradise plays about the expulsion of Adam and Eve from the Garden of Eden. The props were a pine tree for the Tree of the Knowledge of Good and Evil, a snake and an apple. Over the years trees festooned with apples, paper roses and sweets became an established Christmas tradition. In 1880 a German glass maker began to produce decorative baubles, which eventually replaced the real apples.

fruit it referred. In Ancient Greece peaches were known as Persian apples; quince and apricots were golden apples. Several mythological tales feature golden apples. Gaia gave them to Zeus and Hera as a wedding gift to plant in the Garden of Hesperides; one of Heracles' Twelve Labours was to sneak into the garden and take them from the Tree of Life. The Trojan War was sparked indirectly by three goddesses, including Aphrodite, who wished to possess the golden apples which would bestow upon them the title of fairest in the land. They instructed Paris to judge who was

the most beautiful, but Aphrodite bribed him to choose her with the promise of marriage to Helen of Troy.

In Celtic mythology the apple was an emblem of healing and rebirth, and in Norse legend Idun, the goddess of youth, was the keeper of golden apples which gods ate in search of immortality. Symbolically the apple represents beauty, knowledge, fertility, ardour, temptation and loss of innocence, in part due to the association with Aphrodite, goddess of love. In all these tales whether the apple in question is *Malus pumila* is debatable.

ADAM'S APPLE

All humans have an Adam's Apple, the term for a piece of cartilage in the neck that protects the front of the larynx. The name denotes the fruit lodged in Adam's throat after God banished him from the Garden of Eden and is much snappier than its medical term, laryngeal prominence.

Perhaps the best-known apple story is from the Old Testament, where Eve tempts Adam with forbidden fruit plucked from the Tree of the Knowledge of Good and Evil. As punishment for their disobedience God banishes the couple from paradise. The Bible, first written in Hebrew, uses *peri*, a generic term for fruit, but does not mention apples. The Book of Genesis describes Adam and Eve covering their genitals with fig not apple leaves, and Michelangelo's Sistine Chapel fresco of *The Fall and Expulsion from the Garden of Eden* features a serpent coiled around a fig tree. Van Eyck's *The Adoration of the Mystic Lamb* depicts the fruit as a citron, and in Rubens' *The Fall of Man* it is a pomegranate, the name of which stems from Latin for seeded apple, *pōmum grānātum*.

Could the association of *Malus pumila* with evil be linked to a mistranslation of the Bible from Hebrew to Ancient Greek, then Greek to Latin, and later into English? *Mālon*, Ancient Greek for any tree fruit, became *mālum* in Latin. The almost identical Latin *malum* (without the diacritic) means evil. Jerome, a fourth-century Slovenian scholar tasked by Pope Damasus I to translate the Bible from Ancient Greek to Latin, went back to the Hebrew original and interpreted *peri* as *malum* not *mālum*.

In Old English the spelling of apple was *æppla* and it was added as a suffix to other fruits, so what we now call dates were *fingeræppla* (finger apple), and cucumbers *eorþæppla*, or earth apple. Tomatoes were termed 'love apples' when they first appeared in Europe, and the contemporary Italian word for tomato is *pomodoro*, golden apple. The first Latin to English translation of the Bible was published in 1535 as the language was in transition to Modern English. Apple was still the term for all fruit apart from berries, so it is unlikely John Milton was referring to *Malus pumila* in his poem *Paradise Lost*, published 1667, when Satan describes an apple he ate before persuading Eve to do the same.

> To satisfie the sharp desire I had
> Of tasting those fair Apples, I resolv'd
> Not to deferr; hunger and thirst at once
> Powerful perswaders, quick'nd at the scent
> Of that alluring fruit, urg'd me so keene.

In the Old Testament Song of Solomon, however, the apple is believed to symbolise the coming of Jesus Christ: 'As the apple tree among the trees of the wood, so is my beloved among the sons. I sat down under his shadow with great delight, and his fruit was sweet to my taste.' And in the New Testament the apple had a reputational makeover and signified redemption from sin. Renaissance painters were

keen on this symbolism, and numerous works feature the Virgin Mary with the infant Jesus holding a *Malus pumila*. So even though the original biblical fruit was most likely to have been a fig or pomegranate, almost everyone thinks of it as what is now an apple, bestowing a stature no other fruit enjoys.

SACRED PLACES

A SHIMMERING CLOUD in the valley hovers a few metres above ground. Mist? Look closer: it is delicate pink and white apple blossom on dozens of trees in an orchard hidden along a remote track. Birds are singing to proclaim their territory, insects buzz around and sheep graze. It is a little damp, smells earthy, and nature is in full majesty, abundant bucolic splendour in a scene as old as ... not time itself but as old as whenever humans started to manage the landscape and plant orchards, probably in China or Mesopotamia *circa* 4,000 years ago. Ancient Egyptians planted orchards along the Nile. Greeks and Romans embraced the practice too because cultivated fruit was precious, and a walled garden was a status symbol. Fruit cultivation warranted its own deity: Egyptians venerated Renenūtet, Greeks revered Demeter, and Romans worshipped Pomona. Orchards were special, termed *pairidaeza* in Persian, which translated into Latin as *paradises*, the source of the English word paradise. The biblical Garden of Eden was an orchard described as paradise.

PARADISI IN SOLE
Paradisus Terrestris.
or
A Garden of all sorts of pleasant flowers which our
English ayre will permitt to be noursed vp:
with
A Kitchen garden of all manner of herbes, rootes, & fruites,
for meate or sause vsed with vs,
and
An Orchard of all sorte of fruitbearing Trees
and shrubbes fit for our Land
together
With the right ordering planting & preseruing
of them and their vses & vertues
Collected by John Parkinson
Apothecary of London.
1629

Qui veut parangonner l'artifice à Nature
Et nos forces à l'Eden, mesfort il mesure.

Le pas de l'elephant par se pes du citron,
Et de l'Migel se vol par eil du mouscheron.

In Latin, garden is *hortus*, and *geard* was an Anglo-Saxon term that meant enclosure. When combined they became *hortus-geard* and the phrase evolved into English as orchard. For Roman poets they were worthy subjects to write about, and Horace described Italy as being a vast orchard.

When the Romans expanded their influence into Western Europe, they introduced eating apples and orcharding techniques, including grafting. Not much is known about this period of cider history, nor the era that followed the implosion of the Roman Empire in the fifth century, hence its nickname the Dark Ages. In the early ninth century King Charlemagne created the Holy Roman Empire, which covered vast territory in Europe. He established an administrative system with efficient record keeping, and throughout his reign references to cider as the fermented juice of apples appeared. Edicts were issued about the management of royal estates, with instructions on the type of fruit to grow. Specialists called *siceratores* were employed to make wine, beer and cider. As the name Holy Roman Empire suggests, the Catholic Church had great influence, and in Charlemagne's mission to Christianise his dominions, many monasteries were founded, all of which had orchards.

In England medieval records, including household accounts, suggest growing apples was widespread across the land. Some counties are more associated with apples than

ORCHARD MUSEUM

On a farm outside Faversham in Kent, around 4,000 apple, pear, plum, quince, medlar and nut trees make up Britain's National Fruit Collection, one of the world's most extensive. Of that total 2,100 are apples. It is living history and serves as a gene bank to protect the country's fruit inheritance.

others, and English horticulturalist John Evelyn commented in 1664 that 'all Herefordshire is become in a manner but one entire orchard'. International matters influenced cider in the late eighteenth century, when British farmers were pressured to change land use and produce grain and livestock to ensure a domestic supply during the Napoleonic Wars. Countless ancient orchards were destroyed, but Herefordshire refused to lose its apple heritage and today the county still grows more than any other part of the country, with trees on main roads, down remote green lanes, obstinately clinging to valley sides, and solitary pippins grown from apple cores thrown out of passing cars, standing insouciantly in the middle of roundabouts. A walk in the Malvern Hills Area of Outstanding Natural Beauty might reveal gribbles surrounded by dense woodland with tangled undergrowth of ferns, brambles and creepers, reminiscent of how wild *Malus sieversii* grows in Kazakhstan's Tien Shan mountains.

Orchards are domains where nature is the boss, and the growing season cannot be hurried. In springtime trees stage a spectacle, with blossom in full bloom to attract wandering bees and other pollinators to ensure fruit will grow. Bees are indispensable for pollination, and some orchardists keep hives for that purpose. Not all varieties flower at the same time, so the dazzling display continues for several weeks. As trees start to fruit, growers implore the heavens to send the ideal weather conditions of sunlight to intensify sugar levels and rainfall at night to keep the apples hydrated so juice yield will be high. In autumn, trees are heavy with fruit which drops when ripe, thudding into the grass below. A range of cultivars is usually planted because they do not all ripen at once, so harvesting lasts for weeks, which is useful as cider production can be spread out over months. Commercial orchards are harvested either by hand or by shaking the trees. For the latter there are two methods: an implement on a tractor that grabs the trunk and vibrates it, or the low-tech option with a panking pole to hook around a branch for a vigorous quiver. Pickers on their knees hand-sort the fallen apples, or a farm vehicle scoops them onto a conveyor belt and into a trailer. Physical perfection is unnecessary for cider apples so it does not matter if the fruit is blemished during handling. As winter comes orchards look forlorn, and orchardists spend time pruning diseased wood and removing branches to evenly space them so that air and light reach all parts of the tree. Chilly winter temperatures are necessary for trees to enter dormancy and build reserves so the buds will be vigorous in spring for the cycle to begin again.

Cider made from fresh juice rather than concentrate introduces the concept of *terroir* to the flavour profile. The term used in wine making also applies to cider and is the influence of environmental factors. In 1908 Professor B. T. P. Barker, Director of Britain's National Fruit and Cider Research Station, wrote, 'It is inevitable that the nature of the season should exert a considerable influence upon the character of the cider on account of the important part played by sunshine and other weather conditions in connection with the ripening of the fruit.' Climate and weather are not the only factors that affect how apples grow; terroir also includes altitude, wind patterns, direction of sunlight and nutrient content of soils. All can affect acidity and sugar levels. Even apples from trees in other positions in the same orchard could have subtle variations. In Herefordshire this led to the 'A Sense of Place' project by Little Pomona Cidery, when in 2022 they collaborated with seven growers located in the county who each submitted Dabinett apples to be made into single-variety ciders. The apples were processed separately but in the same manner,

and when the seven ciders were blind tasted, the results showed differences in aromatics, flavour and texture. Yet another magical factor about fresh-juice cider.

In literature orchards are often symbolic of being safe places with happy memories. In Anna Sewell's *Black Beauty*, the eponymous character (a horse) says:

My troubles are all over, and I am at home; and often before I am quite awake, I fancy I am still in the orchard at Birtwick, standing with my old friends under the apple trees.

Poet William Wordsworth wrote in 'The Green Linnet':

> Beneath these fruit-tree boughs that shed
> Their snow-white blossoms on my head,
> With brightest sunshine round me spread
> Of spring's unclouded weather,
> In this sequestered nook how sweet
> To sit upon my orchard-seat!
> And birds and flowers once more to greet,
> My last year's friends together.

In *Cider with Rosie*, Laurie Lee's memoir about his rural childhood in a post-First World War Gloucestershire village, Lee writes:

> Never to be forgotten, that first long secret drink of golden fire, juice of those valleys and of that time, wine of wild orchards, of russet summer, of plump red apples, and Rosie's burning cheeks. Never to be forgotten, or ever tasted again...

Orchards are distinct, precious spaces, habitats for birds, insects, amphibians and small mammals, so losing them diminishes biodiversity. Some artisan cider makers are adopting and maintaining abandoned groves and finding forgotten apple varieties, some of them local to that immediate area and nowhere else. Ecological activists in the UK are planting apple trees in underused urban spaces to create wildlife terrains and bring communities together in a natural setting, recognising the truism that orchards are good for the environment and good for the soul.

FROM WHERE TO HERE

WHERE AND WHEN was cider first made? No one knows, but whoever the first cider makers were warrant plaudits for determination, because unlike soft fruits such as grapes, which, due to the delicacy of their skin and flesh, would naturally turn into alcoholic mush with no assistance, apples are tough and need to be chopped up and pounded or pressed with a heavy weight to release their juice.

Historically humans developed the ability to make wine and beer through trial and error, and it was probably the same with cider. A timeline is impossible without archaeological evidence so hypotheses must be made. Humans have purposely created alcoholic drinks since at least the beginning of the Neolithic era (*circa* 10,000 BCE), as a way of preserving food and to sup for recreation, so if apples were available and someone had the wherewithal to access the juice, the assumption is that rudimentary cider was the next step. Awareness would have happened in stages, starting with eating and enjoying an apple, then working out how to liberate the juice and store it in a container for drinking.

After a few days invisible wild yeasts would ferment some of the sugars, leading to a lowish-alcohol liquid that provided a gentle buzz. Ancient Greeks and Romans had pressing machinery for olives and fruit and also had *Malus pumila*. It is likely they drank cider, but being more demanding and labour intensive to make than wine, it was not the first choice. In locations where apples grew but grapes did not, however, the effort needed to make cider was worth it.

Today's longest-established cider regions of Asturias, Basque Country, Normandy, Brittany and parts of Britain have something in common: Celtish heritage. The Celts, a collection of nomadic tribes who considered apples to be sacred, most likely spread cider making through migration and trade as they roamed through Europe in the first millennium BCE. When the Roman Empire expanded, Celts were subjugated and their lands taken, but cider making continued and was assisted by the technology and agricultural know-how of the invaders.

Normandy has been a Ciderland for centuries. The name derives from medieval Latin *Nortmanni* – 'men of the north' – and refers to the Vikings who took advantage of the power vacuum created by Charlemagne's death in 814 CE. Raiding gangs arrived by sea to loot monasteries in what was then called Neustria. Something about the area suited them – cider perhaps? – so some stayed and assimilated and the region was renamed Normandy. When in 1066 William, son of the Duke of Normandy, crossed the English Channel

Fig. 195. — *Tour à piler* les pommes, et ancien pressoir à cidre de la Normandie.

A, auge circulaire en pierre.
B, roue en bois.
M, *mouton* ou levier de pression.
C, *brebis* ou support de pression.

D, D, montants de bois.
R, vis de bois manœuvrée à la main, et qui fait abaisser l'extrémité libre du levier M.

with an army and was victorious in the Battle of Hastings, he earned the soubriquet The Conqueror. England was already a cider-drinking nation but with the arrival of the Normans, cider making was enhanced by the introduction of tannic apples and heavy-duty pressing equipment.

This era in England saw a fourfold growth in the number of monasteries. They were largely self-sufficient, with arable land, animal husbandry, vineyards and fruit gardens. It was no coincidence cider was so popular among the holy orders because, according to the *Rule of Saint Benedict*, a book written in the sixth century as commandments for monks to live by, wine was rationed but cider was not. Monasteries leased out farmland, orchards and presses, and payment in cider was accepted, which could then be sold for profit. Business activities, church tithes and donations from benefactors enriched monastic communities to the point where the Catholic Church was one of the country's wealthiest institutions and, with its authority over people's souls, the most powerful. And then it all ended. Between 1536 and 1541 King Henry VIII ordered the disbandment of Catholic institutions in a policy known as the Dissolution of the Monasteries. Land was confiscated, assets disposed of, and income expropriated by the Crown. This was not just an attack on the established religion, it was an act of cultural vandalism, with the destruction of architecturally significant buildings and the loss of libraries and irreplaceable manuscripts. Records and documents were lost, including references to cider. This turmoil coincided with the Renaissance, a movement that valued learning, where philosophy, science and appreciation of the natural world were guiding principles. With improved literacy and the invention of the printing press, demand for books surged. Horticulture was a popular subject, with herbalists and botanists publishing their reflections

CYDER OR CIDER?

Today both spellings are used but there is no definitive answer to whether, historically, cyder and cider were different drinks, or if it was a regional variation in spelling.

English academic R. K. French theorises in his book *The History and Virtues of Cyder* that cyder was apple wine of up to 11% ABV consumed by the upper classes, and cider was a lower-alcohol long drink for everyday refreshment.

on fruit. Contemporaneous written accounts described the countryside with particular emphasis on orchards, and some mentioned cider. In *The Description of England* (1577) William Harrison wrote, 'In some places of England there is a kind of drink made from apples which they call cider or pomage…'

Sir John Scudamore, Member of Parliament for Hereford, has a starring role in cider history with the bitter-sweet apple he raised from a pip, later named Herefordshire Redstreak and considered at the time to be the most superior cider apple in England. Agriculturalist John Worlidge published his 1676 treatise *Vinetum Britannicum* in which

Red streak

he detailed each stage of cider making and commented that 'a barrel of Redstreak surpassed the best Spanish and English wines'. Scudamore was well connected in the court of Charles I (r. 1625–1649) and presented casks of his cider to senior courtiers and the monarch. If the gifts were bribes, they worked, and he was appointed by Charles to the prestigious role of ambassador to France. Scudamore proved that cider in England was not just the farmhouse kind consumed in the shires; it was also a drink of Kings.

During the interregnum that followed the English Civil War and execution of Charles in 1649, there was no royal court, so aristocrats retired to their country estates and spent time on the land planting orchards and experimenting with grafting. Raising new apples and making wine-like cider became a noble pursuit. This was a golden period for cider, helped by the Little Ice Age, which altered Western Europe's climate and affected grapes but not apples because they survive in cooler temperatures. Cider thrived where wine did not, and it benefited even more when Oliver Cromwell, England's republican leader, instigated protectionist trade policies that prohibited wines from certain European countries. In response, cider makers created high-ABV ciders, and diarist John Evelyn, author of *Pomona* (1664), wrote, 'Our design is relieving the want of wine by a succedaneum of cider.'

By the eighteenth century fine cider was on upper-class dining tables and in louche London drinking dens sardonically termed 'cider palaces'. Rough-and-ready scrumpy was in cider bars at the docks, and in its heartland common cider, aka ciderkin or small cider, was the rural drink of everyone because it was plentiful and provided the cheapest, most accessible refreshment. When in 1763 the Government, led by John Stuart, Earl of Bute, levied a cider tax to fund the deficit in the Treasury caused by the Seven Years' War with France, it also authorised excise officers to enter and search private property without a warrant. For landowners with orchards cider was lucrative; for smallholders with a few apple trees it was part of their cultural heritage. To country folk it was fundamental not just as a beverage but also as currency for paying rent, church tithes and sometimes labour, and consequently there were riots against the new law. After three years of angry demonstrations that included burning effigies of Bute, mock executions, derogatory pamphlets and lobbying of lawmakers, the Government relented and repealed the tax. Opposition to the Act's draconian measures may have inspired the framers of the US Constitution to include the Fourth Amendment, which states that 'The right of the people to be secure in their persons, houses, papers, and effects, against unreasonable searches and seizures, shall not be violated, and no warrants shall issue, but upon probable cause...'

Britain's industrial revolution transformed the country from a rural to an urbanised society where employees in

An *EXCISEMAN* made out of y^e Necessaries of
Life now **Tax'd** in **Great Britain** except the head which is
a *Knaves* taken from y^e *Court Cards*

When Fame first the Olive Branch held o'er the Land,
Then Plenty we hop'd would have Stretch'd out her hand.
The Poor be reliev'd by the — Blessings of **Peace** ———
The **Taxes** diminish, and **Commerce** increase'd,
That Joy would be seen in each Englishmans Face,
And Mirth and Festivity reign through each Place;
Our Houses and Butts from **Excisemen** be freed,
And **Sawney** return to the Banks of the Tweed.
But those golden Dreams are now vanish'd in Smoke,
Britannia must tamely Submit to the Yoke. ———

Drawn from the Life and Etch'd in Aquafortis.

1 The Head of a Knave, 2 A Bottle of Cyder, 3 Candles, 4 Beer, Wine, Perry and Mum, 5 a Guage, 6 Leather,
7 Sope, 8 Chocolate, 9 Coffee, 10 Tea, 11 Light, 12 Land

Peace 3 Feb. 1763   Cyder Act March, 1763

LIQUID PAY PACKET

The Truck Act entered British law in 1887 and prohibited payment for work in goods rather than coin of the realm. Until then it was standard for rural labourers in some parts of the country to receive a proportion of their wages in ciderkin – up to six pints a day, more at harvest time. Many employers ignored the regulation and into the 1940s the offer of cider was still used as a lure for itinerant workers.

factories and heavy industry needed a liquid pick-me-up after work. Some cider makers adopted mechanisation to increase volumes, and with the expansion of the rail network in the mid-nineteenth century enabling wider distribution, they grew into huge businesses. One of them, Bulmers of Hereford, is now the world's biggest producer.

Understanding the science was key to cider becoming a commodity, but until 1857, when French microbiologist Louis Pasteur discovered that yeast was responsible for the creation of alcohol, how it happened was a mystery. Sugar's conversion to alcohol cannot be seen but the by-products can, with occasional visible bubbles of carbon dioxide and a froth appearing on the liquid's surface as fermentation ensues. No wonder the metamorphosis of liquid into an intoxicant was for thousands of years considered to be supernatural, an endowment from the deities. Pasteur's discovery led to the development of cultured yeast strains and, together with research into chemical and biological processes, this made consistency of quality possible, an essential factor for cider to compete with other alcoholic drinks. This was the start of industrially produced cider in Britain, when large regional companies subsumed smaller ones. After the Second World War some of those cider companies were in turn purchased by brewing corporations, which marketed cider the same way as beer, and it became increasingly estranged from its rural roots.

In the 1960s pale pilsner-style lagers grew in popularity in Britain and cider was considered outmoded by younger drinkers who preferred cold, fizzy and less flavoursome beverages. This was an existential threat and Big Cider needed to maintain customers, so that meant offering them softer, lighter-bodied homogeneous beverages. High-tannin acidic apples did not fit the new way, so some heritage cultivars were no longer suitable, and farmers supplying the giant cider companies were compelled to grow a smaller selection of less tannic apples. This is also when the use of juice concentrate became the norm, and today that is how most commercial cider is made.

TRANSFORMATION

IN CIDERLAND, THAT glass of dry golden nectar with layered flavour depths of fragrant melon, zesty orange peel and candied fruit was most likely produced in small batches in a cidery, where an aromatic mixture of named apples and mustiness is a reminder of the natural provenance of the ingredients. By contrast, macro cider, often made of a blend of unspecified varieties in a high-tech factory, is invariably sweet and fizzy. Both cider-making philosophies start by juicing apples that grew from blossom to ripened fruit, but what happens after that differs considerably.

The earliest cider production entailed pounding apples in a container to collect the juice. Microflora in the fruit and surrounding atmosphere fermented the sugars into alcohol and a few days or weeks later the cider was ready to drink. Today, the intention is the same but techniques have evolved. Apples are ground, aka scratted, to pulp in a milling machine (mill). Some producers macerate it for a few hours to soften tannins and break down cell walls in the flesh to boost juice potential. This can also be done

MEET THE RELATIONS

Wine is marketed by grape or region, and beer has more than 150 recognised styles with globally accepted descriptive terminology. With cider there is no agreed language or parameters of what defines the different types. In the absence of circumscribed styles, it is not easy to make an informed choice without some cider knowledge, so the following broad characteristics of categories are a rough guideline.

EASTERN COUNTIES Ciders are fresh and fruity with low tannins and medium acidity, made from popular eating apples such as Jazz and Discovery. The name refers to the eastern counties of England, but the style is not restricted to that specific area.

FLAVOURED CIDER Cider with additional ingredients including fruit, flowers, honey and spices in whole or syrup form.

FRENCH Brittany and Normandy, the premier cider-making regions in France, are known for rich, fruity, complex and tannic ciders. Keeving is a speciality, so some of them are sweet with low alcohol.

Sagardoa The Basque word for cider – it translates as apple wine. Ciders tend to be highly acidic. Those marked 'Euskal Sagardoa' have Protected Designation of Origin (PDO) status and are made from a range of 115 locally grown apple varieties.

Sidra Natural A Spanish term that translates as natural cider, usually from Asturias. It is still, cloudy and unfiltered, has high acidity and tartness, and must be made from specified local apples.

West Country Full-flavoured, full-bodied complex cider made from tannic and acidic apples historically associated with England's western and south-western counties and parts of Wales. Those types of cider apples grow in other regions too, including Australia and the USA.

by adding pectic enzymes, which significantly speeds the activity. Prior to mechanisation scratting was a laborious task performed by hand with a stick, rock, or mortar and pestle, or by using human or horsepower to turn a stone grinding wheel on an axle around a circular trough.

Centuries-old cider mills still exist in some farmhouse cideries – an impressive example is displayed in the Museo de la Sidra in the Asturian town of Nava, and artefacts in Hereford's Cider Museum are a reminder of how cider was made before modern technology existed.

In cider terms, the answer to the question 'What did the Romans ever do for us?' is the press where weight is applied to the pulp by tightening a screw or levering a beam. The method, still employed by some traditional cideries, entails encasing pulp in synthetic mesh and shaping it into a square known as a 'cheese'; the name possibly derived from pre-plastic days when cheesecloth was used as wrapping. Layers of 'cheeses' are laid on wooden slatted trays, then placed in a press. Hydraulic weight is exerted so the juice runs into a collector tray. The pulp, now termed pomace, can be hydrated then pressed again for residual sugars and fermented to make ciderkin. Spent pomace is used for animal feed, to produce biogas or scattered on the orchard floor as fertiliser, where it may even result in gribbles growing from the seeds it contains.

What happens next is one of nature's most extraordinary actions: fermentation, when individual yeast cells reproduce billions of times, consume sugars in the juice and convert them to alcohol, carbon dioxide and hundreds of aroma and flavour compounds. Depending on the producer, cultured or wild yeasts are employed in cider making. The former, often from strains used in

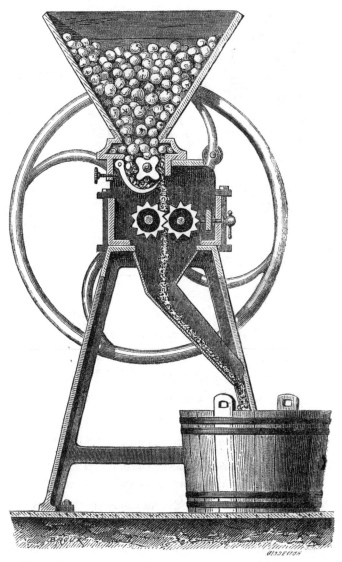

Fig. 194. — Coupe du grugeoir à écraser les pommes.

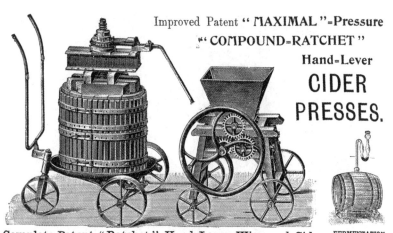

wine making, is fast and reliable. Each cultured yeast cell
is a clone of its mother and predictable in behaviour and
outcome, which is what mainstream cider makers need.
With non-cultured yeast, wild strains live in colonies on
the apple skins and in different parts of the cidery and
can confer indescribable magic in aroma, flavour and
complexity, and impart a unique personality to each cider.

In Ciderland, after fermentation is complete, cider is
aged in tanks or wooden casks, often oak or chestnut, where
it hibernates for months or sometimes years to develop
its character. Some tannic ciders need a couple of years
for the tannins to soften and to taste their best, but acidic
ciders lose their zesty freshness with lengthy ageing and

are best drunk young. A new oak barrel releases vanillin, an aromatic molecule that resembles vanilla, whereas a barrel which previously stored wine or spirits may impart hints of sherry, rum or whisky. At this stage it is dry, a term also used in wine, gin and mead production that denotes absence of sweetness because yeast has consumed the sugars. To make the cider more palatable for a wider audience, it requires back sweetening by adding sugar or unfermented apple juice. It might also need balancing by increasing acidity with the addition of fruit acids, and then blending, where ciders from different maturation vessels are married together. Now it is ready for packaging in bottles, cans, bag in box, or kegs, filtered or unfiltered, possibly pasteurised, still or sparkling.

Cider from freshly pressed juice is made in the months following the harvest, but major brands can produce year-round because they use concentrated apple juice that's available whenever it's needed. Complexity and seasonality are lost by processing juice into concentrate, but it has many commercial benefits, including indefinite storage, fewer production stages, economies of scale and standardised flavour. Juice concentrate producers often employ chaptalising, a system where sugar is added to the juice so it ferments to around 14% ABV, then diluted with water afterwards to reduce the ABV. The reason for doing this is that less juice is required to produce larger volumes of cider. The result is an uncomplicated beverage, usually artificially carbonated and served chilled.

THAT'S THE SPIRIT!

W hen fruit is distilled it becomes *eau de vie*. Distilled cider is often called brandy, and in Normandy and Brittany, where it has *Appellation d'Origine Contrôlée* (AOC) recognition with associated rules of production, it is Calvados and Lambig de Bretagne respectively.

CALVADOS Made from cider apples grown in the Calvados department of Normandy and aged in oak barrels for two years minimum. ABV is at least 40%. *Le trou Normand*, or Norman hole, is a French custom where a shot of Calvados is drunk as a digestif between the courses of a meal.

Lambig de Bretagne Brittany's Lambig de Bretagne, also known as Fine Bretagne, is made from apples grown in Brittany. It must be at least 40% ABV and aged in oak for a minimum of two years.

Mistelle A blend of apple juice and cider brandy aged in oak barrels for months to years. ABV is 16 to 18%.

Pommeau A fortified beverage made by mixing two parts unfermented apple juice with one part Calvados to make Pommeau de Normandie, or adding the same amount of unfermented apple juice to Lambig for Pommeau de Bretagne. Its production is bound by AOC rules. The blend is aged for a minimum of 14 months in oak barrels and ABV is 16 to 18%.

One of cider's advantages is its adaptability in appealing to disparate types of drinkers and drinking occasions, whether glugging a pint on match day, fuelling up at a music festival, celebrating the harvest in a cidery or revering the apple in a wine-like cider at a banquet.

IN ITS OWN SWEET WAY

Cider is not sweet by default, because most sugars convert to alcohol, so how is natural sweetness achieved? Producers have two ways.

KEEVING A complicated production procedure widespread in Normandy and Brittany and used by some producers in England, Australia and the USA. Enzymes are added to juice, and these react with pectin, which forms a thick layer of gel, known in French as *le chapeau brun* (brown hat), on the surface. This starves yeast of nutrients, so it ferments very slowly or ceases completely before the sugars change to alcohol. Keeved cider is primarily made from tannic and acidic apples and is complex, smooth, sweet and lowish in alcohol.

ICE CIDER Ultra-sweet and made either by using frozen apple juice (cryo-concentration) or frozen apples (cryo-extraction). Ice concentrates the juice sugars, which leads to full-bodied ciders with a rich syrup-like mouthfeel (the equivalent of dessert wine). When made of cider apples it will have a tannic backbone with tangy acidity and a sharp clean finish. Alcohol levels typically range from 8 to 15% ABV.

PEAR AND PEAR ALIKE

PERRY, THE UNDER-appreciated cousin of cider, is made from woody-textured, astringent, tannic perry pears, the ugly duckling to the apple's swan. But as the saying goes, if life gives you lemons, make lemonade. Perry producers are alchemists who collaborate with nature and transform the unpromising into something magical; a libation that, depending on pear variety, might be subtle, delicate, fresh, zesty, citrus, fruity, earthy or floral. Pears contain some unfermentable sugars, including sorbitol, which contribute body and a smooth mouthfeel, and they account for perry's underlying sweetness. Like cider, perry comes in the farmhouse style consumed as a long drink, or it can be served as a wine, because some perry is aromatic like Riesling, minerally like Chablis or fruity like Chardonnay.

Pears originated in China and, like apples, their range expanded through animal and human endeavours. Archaeological evidence in the Balkans suggests that during the Neolithic era, in addition to eating the fruit, people used pear trees for firewood, construction, furniture and tools.

Homer's *Odyssey* describes pears, apples and other fruit in the gardens of Alcinous' palace as 'glorious gifts of the gods'. Cultivated pears (*Pyrus communis*) were introduced into Europe by the Romans, and Pliny, who mentioned forty-one known cultivars, also alludes to fermented pear juice in his work *Naturalis Historia*.

Most people have never tasted real perry, not to be confused with pear cider, an industrial product made from sweet dessert pear juice concentrate sometimes confusingly labelled as perry. Artisan perry is rare and special, mostly produced in Britain (the heartlands being Gloucestershire, Herefordshire and Worcestershire), Luxembourg, Germany, and Domfront in Normandy, where it is titled *Poiré*. Austria's region of Mostviertel, which translates as Cider Quarter, has Europe's most extensive unbroken area of pear trees, and there perry is a cultural treasure.

Compared to cider, global perry production volumes are miniscule. The few producers who do make it deserve admiration for their fortitude because everything about the perry pear is a challenge. Perry trees are so slow to grow that the motto 'Plant pears for your heirs' is entirely accurate; a newly planted perry tree will likely need at least twenty years before it presents a bountiful crop. Such unhurried growth means some mammoth-sized trees exist, at least twenty metres tall with equal canopy width. Astonishingly, in certain places centuries-old mother trees of pear varieties still have the vitality to bear fruit.

THE PEAR ESSENTIALS

Perry pears are descended from wildings, which are hybrids of the cultivated pear and the wild pear *Pyrus pyraster*. Like apples, pears do not grow true to type; they vary in aroma, flavour, levels of acidity, tannins, colour (yellow, green, orange, brown, red) and shape (oval, conical, round, elliptical). Some varietal names were inspired by geographical location, or the effect they have on the body, or were named after a person or animal; for instance Beetroot Wick Court Alex, Cowslip, Dead Dog, Flakey Bark, Green Horse, Merrylegs, Mumblehead, Stinking Bishop, Swan Egg, Tumper and Water Lugg.

Regardless of age, perry trees are difficult to harvest because sometimes no fruit at all drops, or it drops in intervals of weeks. Close observation is essential and trees must be harvested just at the right time because in terms of ripeness there is usually no in-between. Fruit can either be very hard and underripe, or too soft. Pears ripen from within, a process called bletting, and quickly become mushy without warning, making them useless for perry because the juice cannot be separated from the solids.

The production of perry is similar to real cider in that the fruit is pressed and the juice slowly fermented and then matured. But perry is demanding for several reasons. Pears need to be macerated for longer than apples, up to two days, to mellow the bitter tannins, and in that time they are susceptible to infection. Pressing is difficult because the flesh does not easily release juice. Perry pears are high in citric acid, hence the astringency, so the juice is prone to changing into vinegar. With all these barriers it is remarkable perry exists at all!

Like cider, perry is sometimes referred to as the English Wine. Throughout decades of war with France, particularly in the eighteenth century, when French wine was prohibited in Britain, perry, cider and port replaced it. With its high acidity and tannins, perry is a champion when matched with food, and because it comes in a number of versions – still, carbonated, naturally sparkling, single-variety, blended, dry, sweet, ultra-sweet nectar-like ice perry (made the way ice cider is) and distilled *eau de vie* – the whole menu from starter to dessert can be paired with something succulent. And if that were not enough, perry has another surprise: in its traditional-method format it resembles Champagne. But delicacy is the watchword, so with food matches avoid intense flavours. Try white fish, shellfish, chicken, pork, egg dishes, risottos, creamy sauces, salads and cheese.

THE IMPRISONED PEAR

Poire Williams is an *eau de vie* made by distilling Williams eating pears. Some producers include a whole pear in the bottle in a technique called *poire prisonnière*. It works by inserting a living bud attached to a tree into a bottle so the fruit grows inside. ABV is 40%.

Perry needs more friends to ensure its existence and safeguard the survival of critically endangered pear varieties, and to reward those magicians who understand the nuances and foibles of such high-maintenance fruit and coax it into something so sublime. The industrialisation of agriculture, where land must return the highest profit, has led to millions of pear trees being felled across Europe, even in perry's heartlands. Supporting perry protects tradition, maintains the landscape by safeguarding ancient trees, ecosystems and biodiversity, and preserves its centuries-long membership of the drinks cabinet.

AN APPLE A DAY

'AN APPLE A DAY keeps the doctor away' is a well-known phrase revised since it appeared in print in 1866 as the Welsh proverb 'Eat an apple on going to bed and you'll keep the doctor from earning his bread.' The aphorism was predated by over a thousand years in 'The Story of Prince Ahmed and the Fairy Paribanou', one of the *Arabian Nights* folktales, in which Ahmed pays 35 gold pieces for a magic apple capable of curing all human disease.

Apples are nutrient dense, high in fibre and rich in polyphenols (from tannins), particularly the peel. Polyphenols have antioxidant and anti-inflammatory properties and activate the immune system. The combination of fibre and antioxidants can moderate cholesterol and high blood pressure and reduce the likelihood of stroke and cardiovascular disease. The pectin content of apples is prebiotic and promotes the development of good bacteria in the gut. Tannic varieties are the most beneficial, and scientific research confirms the existence of high levels of antioxidants in ciders made with that type of apple.

Before modern medicine emerged in the eighteenth century, apothecaries and herbalists recommended plant-based cures. John Gerard wrote of the merits of apples in *Herball, or, Generall Historie of Plantes*, published in 1597, and suggested drinking 'lamb's wool', a concoction of mulled cider and ale. He also praised a combination of apple pulp, lard and rosewater as a moisturiser for beautifying the face. Nicholas Culpeper, writing in the mid-seventeenth century, considered roasted apples to be 'good for the asthmatic; either raw, roasted or boiled, good for the consumptive, in inflammations of the breasts or lungs. Their syrup is a good cordial in faintings, palpitations, and melancholy.' John Evelyn wrote that cider 'excites and cleanses the stomach, strengthens digestion and infallibly frees the kidneys and bladder from breeding the gravel stone'.

Scurvy is caused by vitamin C deficiency and was the scourge of sailors when absence of fresh food on prolonged voyages made them susceptible to the debilitating disease. It was termed 'the plague of the sea' and symptoms included lethargy, bruising, bleeding gums and convulsions. Over the centuries it killed more mariners than anything else, including shipwrecks, armed conflict and all other diseases combined. Basque seafarers dominated European whaling and cod fishing in the

sixteenth century and lengthy transoceanic journeys took them from the tip of South America to Newfoundland in the northern Atlantic. Scurvy ravaged other nations' crews, but those on Basque vessels escaped. The reason? Cider is the Basque national drink, and sailors drank up to a quart each day. No one understood why cider was efficacious, but John Worlidge noted in his 1676 *Vinetum Britannicum*, 'For its specific virtues there is not any drink more effectual against the scurvy.' He also wrote about cider's other health benefits: '… the constant use of this liquor, either simple or diluted, hath been found by long experience to avail much to health and long life, preserving the drinkers of it.'

The health benefits of cider were not just considered to be in the glass, and John Beale, scientist and Fellow of the Royal Society, was prescient about trees when he wrote

DRINK
WHITEWAY'S
"WOODBINE BLEND"
DRY CYDER
and Enjoy your Medicine
for
Rheumatism & Gout
AGENT :
CHARLES WATKINS
THE QUADRANT, CLIFTON

in 1652 that Herefordshire's apple orchards 'do not only sweeten, but also purifie the ambient aire which I conceive to conduce very much to the constant health and long lives, for which our county has always been famous'.

Cider vinegar has long had the reputation of being advantageous for health. It starts as cider, then acetobacter bacteria consume the alcohol and convert it to acetic acid (vinegar). Unfiltered and cloudy cider vinegar contains the 'mother' with proteins, enzymes and good bacteria. As well as being a useful condiment, it boosts the absorption of minerals from food, has antimicrobial properties, can help reduce body weight and manages blood sugar levels by slowing the conversion of carbohydrates.

Excessive alcohol consumption can be harmful to health, but in some cases, as reported in the *British Medical Journal*, moderate drinking might be effective in reducing the risk of ischaemic strokes, high blood pressure and heart disease. Add the properties of apples in preventing the same conditions and some might say real cider has superpowers. Alcoholic drinks are often described as containing 'empty calories', meaning they have no nutritional value, but those that are made from fermented foodstuffs go through biological ennoblement, which enhances nutrition and increases polyphenol bioavailability and activity. Fermented food and drinks are probiotic and contain valuable

Of all the gifts of God to man,
Water excels the rest,
But modesty forbids that I
Should always take the best.

microflora that support gastrointestinal health. The human intestine contains more than 70% of the body's immune system cells, so a healthy gut is the foundation of overall well-being. In moderation real cider has some helpful physical effects, and according to a study by researchers at Oxford University, having a sociable drink with friends is good for mental well-being. That is why in many languages, the word 'cheers' translates as health. *Sláinte! Salud! Santé!*

TASTEFUL

HERE IS A QUIZ question: Which of the three tasting notes below refer to wine and which are artisan cider?

- Straw hued, apricots and tangerine on the nose and palate, with gentle tannins, depth of flavour, and a long dry finish.
- Soft peachy notes, floral with a herbal hint, cleansing acidity and a light body.
- Lemon zest and elderflower aromatics, flavours of pear and stone fruit, and a good length.

Answer: All three are ciders.

In cider tasting, aroma, flavour, acidity, tannins, texture, balance and body are the things to consider. Apple variety, cider-making traditions, terroir, intention and skills of the producer, yeast strain, maturation vessel and duration of ageing are all influential. Cider from eating apples is usually fruity, light-bodied and soft on the palate, whereas cider apples impart complexity and length of finish (how long the

flavours remain on the tongue after swallowing) and lead to a fuller body and texture. Just as most wine does not taste of grapes, not all ciders taste of apples.

To taste like a pro start by choosing an artisan cider and a suitable glass – the best shape has a bowl for aromas to develop and is narrower at the neck to funnel them towards the nose. Then engage the senses:

SIGHT Look at overall appearance, colour and clarity.

SMELL Swirl the cider, then sniff it a few times and try to identify the aromas. The brain registers up to 80% of flavour through the nose.

TASTE Take a sip and let it cover the tongue to stimulate the taste buds. They recognise sour, sweet, salt, bitter and savoury, aka umami. As cider warms in the mouth, aromas are released and travel into the nose where olfactory cells send messages to the brain. Swallow it, then breathe out through the nose and think about flavours and aftertaste. This is retro-nasal tasting.

MOUTHFEEL This combines with the other sensory factors and includes *texture* – is it smooth, chewy or crisp? *Body* – light, medium or full? *Astringent* – is it drying?

TANNINS Are they soft or firm? Do they leave a textural impression on the tongue?

ACIDITY Tangy, sour, tart or zesty?

CARBONATION Is it gentle or tingly, moussey and mouth-filling, or prickly?

ALCOHOL Tastes and smells sweet and has a warming effect in high levels. It is a flavour enhancer, and usually higher strength means a more flavoursome cider.

SERVING TEMPERATURE Influences perception of the cider because lower temperatures mute aroma and reduce sensitivity to flavour and mouthfeel.

A range of six diverse ciders is ideal for a tasting session. It is often hard to describe aromas and flavours, so tasting and discussing them with someone else is helpful. Each person is different in how their senses respond so there are no wrong answers. Real cider ranges in colour from straw, golden and amber to orange and burnt sienna, and tasting descriptions include citrus, caramel, marmalade, spice, tropical, stone and berry fruits, floral, nutty, vanilla, demerara sugar, honey and more.

For best results they should not be chilled too heavily. Start with the driest, most acidic and work up through body and ABV, then finish with a sweet cider. And don't forget the perry!

LET THE GOOD TIMES ROLL

CHAMPAGNE HAS AN unrivalled ability to create anticipation and lighten the mood. Pop a cork and the party commences. Three cheers to Dom Perignon the French Benedictine monk, born in 1638, who is credited with the invention. Except he never claimed that distinction. He *was* a wine maker based at an abbey in the Champagne region but would have worked to prevent bubbles rather than encourage them, because in his era if a wine was sparkling it was considered to be faulty. In warm temperatures yeast could ferment residual sugars, creating natural carbonation, and if the wine was in a bottle, pressure would cause the glass to explode. Hence its nickname, *le vin du diable* – the devil's wine.

The accolade for purposely sparkling an alcoholic drink belongs to English cider makers who, in the 1630s, began adding sugar to bottled cider to start a vigorous secondary fermentation. Sir John Scudamore was one of them and considered his Redstreak cider to be first-rate and deserving of an elegant vessel from which to sip it. Visitors to the Museum of London can view the Scudamore flute, a tall narrow glass shaped like an inverted isosceles triangle and engraved with the Scudamore family arms, the letter S and five (probably apple) trees. It was a precursor to the modern-day Champagne flute and dates to *circa* 1635–50.

Another central figure in this story is natural philosopher Sir Kenelm Digby, who, with polymath James Howell, investigated glass making and built on the work of Sir Robert Mansell in the 1620s by pioneering the use of coal for glass production. Coal burned at higher temperatures than charcoal, the usual fuel, and impurities in the coal contributed to resilience in the glass. Digby and Howell developed a furnace that increased the temperature and produced robust dark glass bottles which the French termed *le verre anglais*. Two essential factors in the development of sparkling drinks were sturdy bottles able to withstand immense carbon dioxide pressure within, and an efficient closure to retain carbonation. Digby used cork to seal bottles of sparkled cider and wrote about it in his book, *The Closet of the Eminently Learned Sir Kenelme Digbie Knight Opened*, first published in 1669. He suggested the most effective way of storing bottles was to place them in sand to keep cool, thereby preventing explosions in summer, and to insulate them with hay so they did not freeze in winter.

In 1660 the Royal Society was founded in London as a scientific academy for investigating the natural world. Its archives contain papers and correspondence about

THE
CLOSET
Of the Eminently Learned
Sir *Kenelme Digby* Kt.
OPENED:
Whereby is DISCOVERED
Several ways for making of
Metheglin, Sider, Cherry-Wine, &c.
TOGETHER WITH
Excellent Directions
FOR
COOKERY:
As also for
Preserving, Conserving, Candying, &c.

Published by his Son's Consent.

London, Printed by *E. C.* & *A. C.* for
H. Brome, at the West End of
St. *Pauls*, 1671.

WAYS TO SPARKLE CIDER

The *méthode champenoise* – aka Champagne method, *méthode traditionelle* (traditional method) or *méthode classique* (classic method) – is just one way of adding sparkle to cider and wine, but it is the most prestigious and complicated, and takes the longest time. Other techniques are:

- Bottle conditioned: Secondary fermentation in the bottle after the addition of more yeast before it is sealed. Yeast ferments the sugars and causes gentle natural carbonation. The lees sink to the bottom and remain in the bottle.
- *Charmat*, aka Tank Method: Cider is stored in pressurised stainless-steel tanks and a secondary fermentation is induced. Prosecco is made this way.
- *Pétillant naturel*, aka Pet Nat: A French term that translates as 'naturally sparkling'. Cider finishes its first fermentation in the bottle with the creation of delicate bubbles. Also termed *méthode ancestrale*.
- Forced carbonation: Carbon dioxide from a gas canister is infused directly into the cider.

cider and wine, including one from Captain Silas Taylor, gentleman cider maker and antiquary, who in 1663 outlined how he placed bottled cider in cold water to make it 'drink quick and lively, it comes into the glass not pale or troubled but bright yellow, with a speedy vanishing nittiness [full of small bubbles] which evaporates with a sparkling and whizzing noise'.

Sparkling cider was so alluring that wine dealers in London did the same to still white wines imported from northern France. They were decanted from wooden barrels into reinforced English glass bottles, then sugar was added and they were sealed with a cork. An airtight seal had the bonus effect of preventing bacteria entering and turning the contents to vinegar, with CO_2 playing a role by thwarting oxygen ingress, thus bottled sparkling cider, and wine, was reliable in maintaining quality. Scientist and physician Christopher Merret submitted a paper to the Royal Society in 1662 in which he described how 'our wine coopers of recent times use vast quantities of sugar and molasses to all sorts of wine to make them brisk and sparkling'. The date is evidence that Champagne, an evolution of sparkled cider, was not a French innovation, also confirmed by the late-seventeenth-century description in France of sparkling wine being made in the 'English fashion'.

Champagne became a source of French pride in the early nineteenth century, in no small part due to Barbe-Nicole Ponsardin Clicquot, more familiar as the

Widow (Veuve) Clicquot, who experimented with various practices that became known as *méthode champenoise*. One of them involved racking bottles at an angle so dormant yeast cells would gather in the neck and were easier to remove, a procedure described in connection with cider by John Worlidge in *Vinetum Britannicum* more than 130 years earlier.

Just over a century after Dom Perignon's death in 1715, a monk from the same abbey at Hautvillers erroneously claimed Perignon had invented sparkling wine. An internet search will return thousands of results that concur, many of which include the quotation attributed to him but which he never said: 'Come quickly brothers! I am tasting stars!' That was a nineteenth-century advertising slogan for a Champagne brand.

Champagne borrowed from seventeenth-century cider makers, and twentieth-century cider makers borrowed back. In 1906 Bulmers of Hereford released Cider de Luxe made in the *méthode champenoise* (nowadays referred to as the traditional method in English). Percy Bulmer, co-founder of the company, had spent time in France learning the skills. Cider de Luxe was later named Pomagne and until 1975 marketed as Champagne cider. Bollinger sued the company to prevent it using the word Champagne but lost the lawsuit. Bulmers ceased using the term regardless due to production changing from bottle to bulk tank fermentation.

Cider made in the traditional method starts with a decision on which apple varieties to use. The juice is fermented and the cider bottled with yeast and sugar to trigger a secondary fermentation, then sealed with a crown cap and left to age and improve for months or years in a dark, cool cellar. Towards the end of the maturation period, bottles are tipped at an angle in a rack and gently 'riddled', i.e. rotated either by hand or machine. Yeast sediment, aka lees, settles in the neck, which is then frozen. Once opened

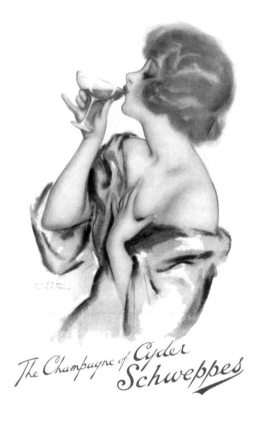

The Champagne of Cyder
Schweppes

CO_2 pressure forces out the ice plug of lees in the process of disgorgement. The bottle is quickly sealed with another crown cap or a Champagne cork. When it comes to serving it, unless the drinker is a wine expert they may have no idea they are drinking sparkling cider and not Champagne. The resulting drink is dry, complex, with a moussey texture, and far too good to waste smashing a bottle of on the bow of a launching ship!

FEASTING WITH CIDER

CIDER COMES IN several versions – still, sparkling, tannic, acidic, dry, sweet and ultra-sweet – so it has great scope for enhancing myriad dishes.

It is tempting to ponder which foods go well with apples, but when pairing wine the consideration is not what matches grapes; instead tannins, acidity, sweetness, carbonation or lack of, and level of alcohol guide the choices. It is the same with cider, and this is why:

TANNINS These are organic compounds found in tea, coffee, cereals, nuts, some vegetables and most fruits. In apples they are in the skins, stems, seeds and flesh and contribute bitterness, astringency and structure. Their presence in liquids performs a useful role because they act like magnets to attract fat and proteins. This helps to cut through the texture of dense or fatty food and refresh the mouth.

ACIDITY Apples contain fruit acids. They are refreshing, heighten the perception of flavour, cut through heavily

MATCHING MANTRA

CO-ORDINATE Think about the texture, density and flavour intensity of food and match with an appropriate-bodied cider.

CUT Choose cider with tannins, acidity or both, to cut through texture, flavour, richness and fattiness. Carbonation also has a cutting effect.

COMPLEMENT Choose a cider to complement the food's flavours, density or texture.

CONTRAST Choose a cider to contrast with the food's flavours.

textured or oily food, and cleanse the palate. Acidity in cider has a mouth-watering effect caused by salivary glands, and this is an appetite stimulant.

SWEETNESS Sweetness acts as a contrast to savoury and salty food and also calms spiciness.

CARBON DIOXIDE Astringent and efficient at cutting through the texture of food, scrubbing the mouth and making it ready for another morsel.

ALCOHOL A flavour enhancer. High-ABV ciders work for full-flavoured food and lower-ABV ciders for delicate dishes.

MATCHING TIPS

- Think about the food's texture. Serve flaky white fish with lighter-bodied ciders, and firm venison with a full-bodied tannic cider, for example.
- Consider how the food is cooked and choose a cider accordingly. For instance, a fried dish would be better with tannins and acidity, while something steamed would suit a light-bodied acidic cider.
- Match cider with the main part of the dish rather than the accompaniments, unless it has a dominant sauce, in which case think about those flavours.
- Alcohol is a flavour enhancer, so higher-ABV ciders will intensify the food and can make it taste unpleasant. Avoid high-alcohol ciders with spicy food.
- Salty foods can make cider taste bitter. Salt clashes with tannins in cider but works well with acidity.
- Savoury foods can make tannic ciders taste bitter so choose acidic or fruity ciders instead.
- Bitter foods – avoid tannic cider as it will increase bitterness.
- Spicy foods – avoid tannic cider as tannins increase spiciness.
- Sweet foods – cider should be sweeter than the food otherwise the cider will taste bitter.

CIDER BANQUET

This is a real combined menu from two separate state banquets at Buckingham Palace and Windsor Castle in honour of the sitting French president at the time. Wine was served with each course and is noted below, but if this meal had been hosted in Ciderland, guests would instead have imbibed the suggested cider and perry.

SOUP COURSE
Cream of asparagus
WINE Baron de L Pouilly Fumé,
Patrick de Ladoucette 2002
PERRY Bottle-conditioned dry perry
WHY The perry has a delicate floral flavour that complements the asparagus and astringency to balance the richness of the soup.

STARTER
Fillet of brill
WINE Marquis de Laguiche Montrachet Grand Cru,
Joseph Drouhin, 2000
CIDER Single-variety Foxwhelp
WHY The cider is dry with high acidity, citrus and herbal notes. Lemon and fish are perfect partners. It also works because brill has a sweetness that contrasts with the cider's zestiness.

MAIN COURSE
Lamb with artichokes and broad beans, cauliflower with Hollandaise sauce, carrots with tarragon
WINE Premier Grand Cru Classé,
Chateau Margaux 1961
CIDER Single-variety Kingston Black
WHY Tannins and acidity cut through the
lamb's fatty texture.

DESSERT
Rhubarb cake with vanilla cream
WINE Krug Champagne 1982
CIDER Keeved bittersweet cider aged
in whisky barrels
WHY Its sweetness is a contrast to the tangy
rhubarb. Vanillin from the oak barrel
is complementary.

CHEESE COURSE
Blue Stilton
WINE Château Guiraud,
Premier Cru Sauternes 2002
PERRY Ice perry
WHY Perry and blue cheese have a magical
affinity. The perry is rich and fruity
and its sweetness contrasts with the
saltiness in the cheese.

JOLLIFICATIONS

IMAGINE WALKING INTO a cathedral but rather than pews the nave is lined with dozens of huge chestnut casks containing thousands of gallons of cider. Is this heaven? Yes, heaven on Earth, and the cathedral is a cavernous cidery in Asturias where cider is a secular religion and source of national pride.

Verdant Asturias, on the Atlantic coast of northern Spain, is one of the world's original Ciderlands. Visiting a cidery to taste *sidra natural*, unfiltered, uncarbonated and highly acidic, served directly from a gigantic cask, is one of the traditions. Drinkers queue up next to the *escanciador* (the person pouring), who opens a spigot from which cider gushes into a glass held at arm's length. Doing this rouses the dissolved CO_2, imbuing a moussey texture. Each measure, or *culín*, is short, just enough for a gulp, so frequent refills are necessary. This is the technique of *escanciar*, which means 'throwing the cider'. Not all of it lands in the glass, so the air is perfumed and the floor sticky. *Escanciar* not only happens in the cidery but every time *sidra natural* is served from

SIDRA CHAMPAGNE
DE
VILLAVICIOSA
(Asturias.)
Valle Ballina
y Fernández
LIT. MORÉ HERMANOS Y Cª GIJÓN

¡FELIZ NAVIDAD!

Argentina, a major apple-growing nation, is not well known globally for its cider, but spend the Christmas season there and it is impossible to avoid. Cider is *the* toasting drink on Christmas and New Year's Eve, and for celebrating at the family dinner when chilled, sparkling sweet cider is served with dessert.

a bottle, when a certain attitude is required to perform it. Stand with a straight back, feet apart and hold the bottle by extending a straight arm above the head. With glass in hand at hip level in line with the navel, tilt the bottle so a stream of cider lands in the glass and awakens the carbonation, then quickly swallow the *culín* before it dwindles.

To celebrate the release of new-season cider, the annual Primer Sidre l'Añu (First Cider of the Year) festival is held in the city of Gijón. It coincides with the four days of Easter, and bagpipers and drummers in Asturian national costume lead crowds through the streets to a showground where dozens of cider makers unseal their barrels of *sidra natural* after months of ageing. The wooden plug is called an *espicha*, and this lends its name to a communal meal consisting of pork shoulder, chorizo, Spanish omelette, hard-boiled eggs, pies and cheese. To complete the *espicha*, pipers play, and *tonadas*, Asturian folk songs, are sung. On Good Friday the Via Crucis (Way of the Cross) procession takes hours to reach the showground because it stops off for eating and drinking at numerous cider houses along the route.

No organised cider happening would be complete without the presence of the Buena Cofradía de los Siceratores (Good Brotherhood of the Siceratores). They act as informal ambassadors for Asturian cider and gastronomy and are recognisable in calf-length green woollen cloaks (as a nod to the green glass of local cider bottles), adorned on the inner edge with a strip of golden yellow velvet the colour of cider, and a medallion which denotes the head of a barrel. The outfit is topped by a *montera picona*, the Asturian green felt hat with two pointed vertical tips, a symbol of the region.

Festivals happen year-round, with *escanciar* contests and a prize for the best homemade cider. For the latter the winner is crowned with a cork version of the *montera picona*. Some festivals include a cider song contest for the best performer of *cancios de chigre*, ditties typically sung in the past by well-oiled customers in cider houses, with lyrics on the theme of local culture and, of course, the liquid that runs through the veins of every Asturian: *sidra*.

Basque Country, east along the coast from Asturias, also has an ancient cider culture. The period between January

and April is the *txotx* season when *sagardotegi* (cider houses) invite people to sample *sagardoa*, that year's new cider. *Txotx*, pronounced 'chotch', translates as toothpick and refers to the bung in a cider barrel. Cider drinking is accompanied by a feast of chorizo, cod omelette, beef steak, local cheese, quince jelly and walnuts. Diners stand at high tables to eat so they are ready to queue up when they hear the cry of 'Txotx!' That is the signal a barrel is about to

THE HESSIAN WAY

Think Germany, think beer? Maybe, but in the state of Hessen *Apfelwein* (apple wine) is the national drink and its production and traditions are included in UNESCO's Intangible Cultural Heritage of Humanity register. Frankfurt's cobbled old town in Sachsenhausen is the cider district, where timber-framed taverns display floral wreaths at the entrance, a modern-day replica of the foliage that historically hung above the door to signal a delivery of fresh cider. Dry and tart *Apfelwein* is served from *Bembels*, blue and grey patterned stoneware jugs, and poured into ribbed glasses called *Geripptes* etched with diamond shapes. A *Deckelchen*, small wooden lid, covers the jug to prevent flies landing on the cider. Together this trio of devices is *das magische Dreieck*, the magic triangle.

Apfelwein is consumed with the local delicacy *Handkase mit Musik* – gelatinous cheese, chopped onions, vinegar and oil, spread on buttered pumpernickel bread and sprinkled with caraway seeds.

be opened from which a stream of dry, acidic cider pours, enlivening the CO_2 as it hits their glass. This happens repeatedly throughout the evening because in Basque the philosophy is to drink 'little and often'.

In parts of Britain, instead of saying 'Cheers' it is customary to say 'Wassail', a word that evolved from the Anglo-Saxon term *wæs þu hæl*, which meant 'be thou hale'. Wassail refers not only to the salutation, but also to a gathering of people in orchards who beseech the spirits to ensure a good harvest, a traditional English activity practised on Twelfth Night that originated in the medieval era. Each region had its own customs, including a wassail bowl containing cider spiced with ginger, cinnamon and cloves taken around the orchard to bless the trees. Roman naturalist Pliny commented, 'The apple tree is the most civilised of all trees' and, seeing regimented lines of grafted trees, it is easy to agree, but there is also something anarchistic and individualistic about an apple tree, because left to its own devices it would grow wherever it wanted. Wassailing perfectly suits that devil-may-care attitude. Nowadays it happens on or around 5 January or 17 January, aka Old Twelvy, Twelfth Night before the Gregorian calendar was adopted in England in 1752. Some wassailers have painted faces, wear foliage around their hats, and are dressed in clothing trimmed with moss-coloured ribbons to represent the Green Man, a symbol of rebirth and the coming spring. By the light of flaming torches, the Wassail

King and Queen lead the parade and gather round a chosen tree, known as Apple Tree Man, in which the orchard's fertility resides. Cider is poured onto the roots, and pieces of cider-soaked bread are hung from its boughs to attract birds, which contain good spirits. To stir the orchard from its slumber everyone makes a hullabaloo by shouting, drumming, or beating pots and pans before gunshot from a rifle is fired through the crown of Apple Tree Man to scare off evil forces. Finally, a toast is downed, everyone shouts 'Wassail', and then the party really starts, often with Morris dancing, singing and of course more cider. Cider drinking is more enjoyable when consumed in company. Add in some ritual and it tastes even better.

REVIVAL

WHAT A TIME TO be a fan of real cider because this is another golden age. A proliferation of cideristas are honouring the apple at cider clubs where people meet producers and taste their wares, exploring cider tourism trails, flocking to food-matching events in cidery taprooms and visiting international festivals to share the love. This has prompted that most powerful of motivating forces, the FOMO (fear of missing out) factor, which only happens if there is significant enthusiasm about something. If proof were needed, look at cider social media, where passion jumps from the screen.

A number of factors combined in the 1990s and contributed to cider's renaissance in countries where juice concentrate makers dominate the market: a surge of celebrity TV chefs, foodie culture, an interest in cooking and baking, the rise of the conscientious drinker, and the slow food movement, which works to protect localism and natural culinary traditions and eschews highly processed industrialised comestibles. At the same time, Big Cider had

a problem because among younger drinkers it was uncool. In Britain this changed in the early twenty-first century when an Irish company introduced Magners with slick TV adverts featuring attractive young professionals quaffing cider in picturesque countryside glades. At first only available in bottles, bar staff were instructed to serve it over ice because a pint glass filled with ice cubes did not have space to hold all the cider, so customers had to take the bottle to their seat where others would notice what they were drinking. It was priceless product placement and Magners was suddenly ubiquitous, recasting cider as an aspirational beverage that appealed to a new generation of drinkers.

Arguably the most dramatic cider revival happened in the USA, where the apple is a signifier of the nation: 'as American as apple pie', as the saying goes. To explain why means looking back to the earliest days of European settlement when English colonists planted orchards as a food source and a reminder of home. Apples grown from pips rather than by grafting suited local environmental conditions and this led to great diversity. The fact that not all seedlings were edible was no problem when fruit was made into cider. As settlers moved west, in exchange for a land grant they were required to plant at least 50 apple or pear trees to demonstrate their intention to remain there. Fortunately for them John Chapman, an entrepreneurial orchardist, had gone ahead and planted nurseries so saplings were available for purchase. Apple trees were low

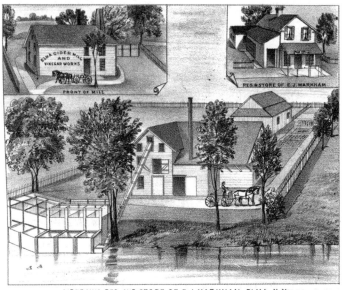

CIDER MILL RES. AND STORE OF E.J.MARKHAM, ELMA, N.Y.

maintenance and could grow on terrain not suitable for other crops. Chapman, better known in American folklore as Johnny Appleseed, is the reason why apples became so prolific throughout the continent, with thousands of varieties at the peak. Anyone with an orchard usually made cider for domestic consumption and for a couple of centuries it was the national drink, supped by almost everyone.

A preference for beer developed in the late nineteenth century with mass immigration from Germany and the Czech Republic. America was becoming an industrialised nation, prompting an exodus from the countryside into towns and cities. Cider, the rural drink, was left behind, and

NOT YOUR
QVEVRI-DAY CIDER

Georgia in the Caucasus is one of the world's oldest wine cultures, dating back around 8,000 years. It has a singular method of fermenting and maturing wine using large egg-shaped terracotta *qvevri*. They resemble amphora without handles, hold up to 900 gallons and are often buried in sand or gravel with their collar poking out of the earth to maintain a stable temperature.

Some USA-, UK- and Finland-based wine makers with *qvevri* have been inspired to use them for making cider. Apple juice is poured in, then the lid sealed with beeswax. Wild yeast slowly ferments the juice for months and eventually lees drop into the vessel's pointed base, leaving the fermented cider on top to be decanted. There is rarity value to these ciders because the process is fiddly and time-consuming, but they profit from contact with the clay because it imparts bright fruitiness, minerality and an earthy savoury character.

instead beer, which was more readily available, became the first choice. Around that time the burgeoning temperance movement spread the belief that alcohol was a malign influence on society, and that rather than drinking apples, they should be eaten. This spurred many orchardists to switch to growing dessert apples. Anti-alcohol crusaders achieved their goals when in 1919 the National Prohibition Act passed into law and the US Constitution was revised, with the Eighteenth Amendment stipulating:

> … the manufacture, sale, or transportation of intoxicating liquors within, the importation thereof into, or the exportation thereof from the United States and all territory subject to the jurisdiction thereof for beverage purposes is hereby prohibited.

Cider apple orchards were burned down by zealous teetotallers or grubbed up, with the loss of countless heritage cultivars. When Prohibition was repealed in 1933 and it was once again legal to produce cider, there were problems. The most widely available apples were grown for eating and did not make good cider, and even if cider apple trees were planted they would take several years to be productive. Furthermore, a generation that had grown up never having tasted cider had soft drinks and carbonated light-flavoured beers from the giant brewers as alternatives. And that's how it was for a few decades until craft beer emerged in the late 1980s, with independent brewers prioritising flavour, and the use of whole ingredients. It gained a following of passionate advocates who welcomed innovation and who were seeking something distinctive rather than a standardised industrial commodity. Real cider benefited from how craft beer influenced the drink sector, especially in satisfying consumer desire to know how food and drink is produced and from what. Despite the loss of apple diversity wrought by Prohibition, some old cider apple trees had hung on, forgotten or ignored on the fringes, along roadsides or hidden in gardens; they have now been grafted so there is a reliable supply. New-wave cider makers have the necessary materials, determination and adventurous spirit, which is attracting converts by challenging the mainstream opinion of what cider is supposed be. Cider infused with Lapsang Souchong tea smoked over pinewood; cider co-fermented with damsons or cherries, then aged in former tequila barrels; cider blended with brown rice, almonds and cinnamon for a creamy, nutty, spicy mash-up. Traditionalists may have a conniption at the thought of these new-wave concoctions but there are still elegant, acidic, Champagne-like ciders, and ciders made with a blend of tannic apples and nothing else dispensed from an oak cask in a farm shop.

No artisan producer ignores the unequivocal fact that apples are the perpetual core of their craft and offer possibilities and intrigue that juice-concentrate ciders cannot. The UK's Ross-on-Wye Cider and Perry celebrated this maxim with the One Juice project, which examined nature over nurture by giving five cideries the same blend of juice from apples grown in one orchard. The idea was for them to ferment and age the juice using their own cider-making philosophies and the results were startlingly varied – from bone dry, to sweet (one had been keeved), spicy from the strain of yeast, to smoky, having been matured in a former Islay whisky cask.

Artisan cider is still a tiny percentage of the overall market but it is slowly expanding as inquisitive drinkers are converted by what that seemingly commonplace little fruit, the apple, is capable of, and professional drinks journalists discover why insiders have been rhapsodising for years. Mother Nature has gifted humans a precious jewel. Wassail!

GLOSSARY OF TERMS

Alcohol by Volume The amount of alcohol contained in 100ml of cider expressed as a percentage. Abbreviated as ABV.

Applejack An American high-strength cider produced since the late seventeenth century made by freezing, or jacking, cider and removing the ice to concentrate the alcohol. ABV varies between 30 and 50%.

Apple Juice Concentrate Juice is heated so 90% of the water evaporates and creates a stable syrup, with long-term storage potential, to be diluted when needed.

Back Sweetening A way to sweeten dry cider by adding sugar or unfermented apple juice.

Balance When all elements of the cider unite without one or more overwhelming the others.

Blending Different apple varieties are mixed before juicing, or the fermented cider is blended to improve structure and drinkability.

Body The feel, texture and sensation in the mouth of cider's fullness, or lack of.

Chaptalisation A technique used by macro cider producers as an inexpensive way of making more cider without the need for extra juice. Sugar is added to juice prior to fermentation to increase ABV so it can be diluted with water to the required lower alcohol level afterwards.

Ciderkin Low-alcohol cider from the second pressing of apple pulp.

Dry When most sugars are fermented from the cider it is classified as dry. That is, absence of sweetness rather than a texture on the tongue.

Gribble A young apple tree grown from a pip. It can also mean immature fruit fallen from the young tree.

Hard Cider In the USA hard cider refers to an alcoholic drink from fermented apples whereas apple cider is raw unfiltered juice that contains no alcohol.

Heirloom American term to describe an apple variety grown for at least 50 years.

Holy Trinity The perfect balance of sweetness, acidity and tannins in an apple.

Lees Dead yeast cells.

Maceration Chopped-up apple pulp rests for a certain time during which cell walls break down, making juice extraction more efficient.

Mill A machine for crushing or chopping apples into small pieces for pressing. Also known as a scratter.

Mouthfeel The sensation of cider in the mouth. It includes carbonation, texture, temperature and body.

Panking Pole A long pole with a hook on the end. Used for hand-harvesting to shake tree branches so apples fall to the ground.

Pippin An apple grown from a pip rather than from a grafted tree.

Pomace Remains of apple pulp after the juice is pressed. Often used for animal feed, fertiliser, or to make biogas.

Press A machine that extracts juice by exerting pressure on apple pulp.

Pulp Chopped, crushed or milled apples for pressing.

Residual Sugar Sugar not consumed by yeast. The lower the residual sugar the drier the cider.

Scrumpy 1. Cider made from apples stolen or 'scrumped' from a tree. 2. Traditional West Country minimal-intervention unfiltered tannic still cider. 3. The cider equivalent of rocket fuel.

Secondary Fermentation A second fermentation in a separate vessel to that of the primary fermentation; for example, maturation tank, wooden barrel, bottle.

Single Varietal Cider made from one variety of apple rather than a blend.

Tannins Compounds derived from organic materials. In cider they are from apples and oak barrels. They provide structure to cider and in high levels are astringent and bitter.

Terroir French term for geographical factors such as soil, location and climate that influence cider character.

Vintage 1. Cider made of apples from a single year's harvest. 2. A marketing term to describe a premium cider.

Yeast Microscopic single-celled fungi that consume sugar and convert it by fermentation to alcohol and carbon dioxide. Some strains also impart aroma and flavour. Large-volume cider makers prefer cultured yeast for speed and predictability. Artisan producers favour wild yeast that lives in the atmosphere and on apple skins.

FURTHER READING

James Crowden, *Ciderland* (Birlinn, 2008)

James Crowden, *Cider Country* (William Collins, 2021)

Ana Maria Vicosia Fuente, Cider Ayalga blog – https://cider ayalga.com

Ian S. Hornsey, *Alcohol and Its Role in the Evolution of Human Society* (Royal Society of Chemistry, 2012)

LIST OF ILLUSTRATIONS

All images from the collections of the British Library unless otherwise stated.

Also available in this series